The Little Angel Books Series

One Red Rose

Written & Illustrated

by Leia A. Stinnett

ISBN 0-929385-83-7

Published by
StarChild Press
a division of
Light Technology
Publishing
P.O. Box 1526
Sedona, Arizona 86339
(520) 282-6523

Printed by
MISSION POSSIBLE
Commercial
Printing
P.O. Box 1495
Sedona, AZ 86339

One Red Rose

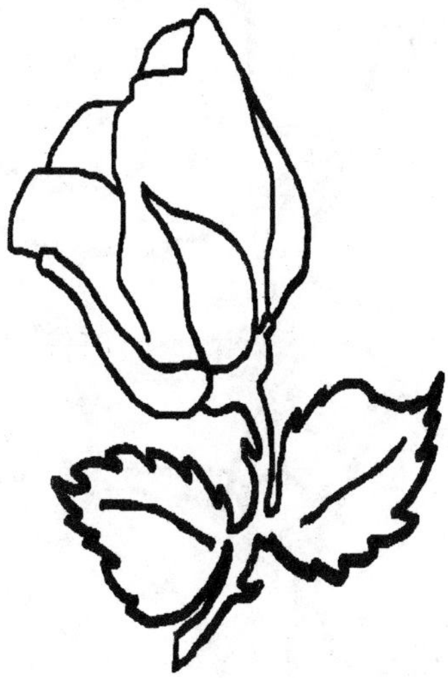

Amy was small for her age, but very, very loving and bright. She had large, crystal clear blue eyes that resembled the sky on a clear summer day.

Her long, blond curls framed her fragile face, which always wore a warm, loving smile for everyone she met. Her grandmother had taught her to love everyone and all of God's Earth. Amy had learned her lesson well.

Regardless of people's beliefs, whether they were rich

or poor, no matter what color their skin, Amy always had a big smile for them all, along with a warm, friendly "hello!"

And Amy had a very special feeling inside for all of God's living things – for the plants, trees and flowers, for the birds, animals and insects, even for the stones and rocks.

Amy's family was very poor. Her father had been ill for several months and unable to work.

With a new baby to care for, Amy's mother had not been able to look for work as well. So the family's income came from the aluminum cans and glass bottles Amy's father collected and sold to the local

recycling center. Amy often accompanied her father in his search for such collectibles. She liked to help as much as she could.

Amy's mother did some sewing for a few of the people who lived in the city. Amy liked to help Mom cut out the patterns or put colorful quilts together.

There was very little money, but the great amount of love the family shared more than made up for what they did not have in the way of material things.

Amy's family lived in a small, rundown neighborhood near the railroad tracks on the west side of town. Most of the townsfolk looked down their noses at the neighborhood.

They felt ashamed of the neighborhood. The townsfolk called Amy's family and her neighbors the "poor" people, thinking they were better because they had fine houses, fancy cars and a lot of nice things.

The townspeople ignored the needs of Amy's neighborhood and did not realize they were all good people in need of a little love, understanding and support in improving their lives. Many of the people in Amy's neighborhood were out of work and unable to afford a better place to live.

Like the other homes in the neighborhood, Amy's house was

old and in need of repair.

Most of the paint had peeled away from the outside over the past few years.

The broken windows were neatly sealed with plastic bags to keep out the cold winter weather.

Amy's father used scraps of wood which he had found in his search for recyclables to mend the badly leaking roof as well as some of the holes in the outside walls.

Though the little house looked tattered and worn on the outside, the inside expressed a feeling of warmth, love and true sharing.

Amy's mother kept the

house neat and clean. She decorated the rooms with "treasures" she had found in thrift stores, and from some of the throwaways of her sewing customers.

She was very creative and always surprised Amy with her ability to design beautiful things from scraps of material she used in her sewing projects.

The house was warm and cozy, with a friendly fire dancing briskly in the fireplace, radiating a warm glow throughout the tiny house.

Amy's parents and little brother slept in the one small bedroom, but Amy felt she had the best bedroom of all.

Next to the fireplace in a

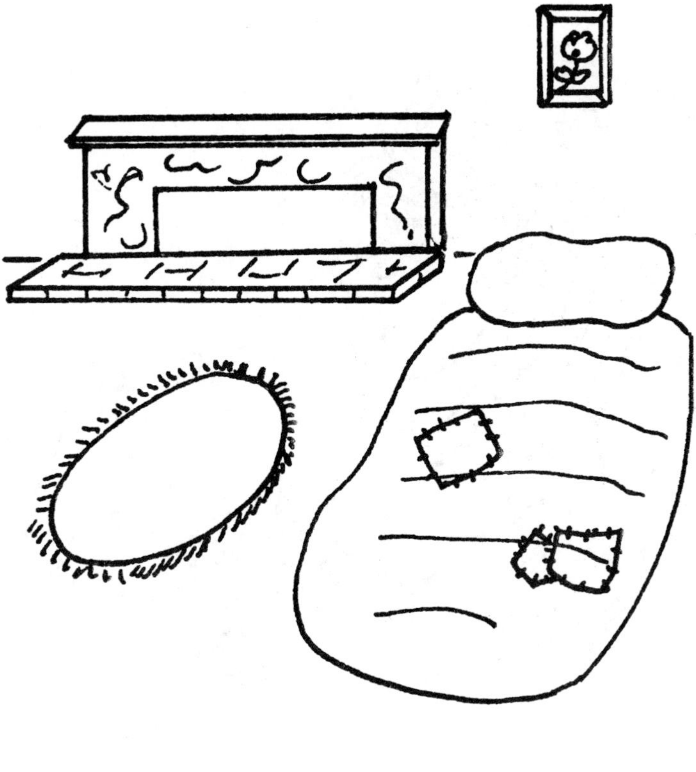

corner of the living room, Amy's mother had placed a small, worn mattress, covered with a colorful, thick, warm quilt her grandmother had made for her just before she passed away.

On the wall above her head was a small picture of one single red rose, another special gift from Grandma.

Grandma said the rose symbolized love and compassion, the kind of love and compassion we should all share openly with all people and all creatures of the Earth.

"Love is a special gift from God. It is a gift we should share with everyone we meet, no matter how they feel or act toward us," Grandma had told her. "Love should come from the heart, giving freely, expecting nothing in return."

Grandma was Amy's best friend. And Grandma's words were important to Amy. She tried very hard to be just like Grandma – loving and kind to everyone, always cheerful and happy.

Because they were poor, Amy did not have nice clothes and a lot of toys to play with. However, her mother had made her a very special doll from scraps of colorful sewing materials.

Amy named her doll Lea. Lea had a cute little round face and gold yarn for hair.

Two large blue buttons formed Lea's eyes. In fact, Lea looked a lot like Amy.

Amy and Lea were very close. Amy took Lea everywhere she went, as they were the best of friends.

When Amy went to school, she found the other children very unfriendly toward her. They always made fun of her clothes and the neighborhood in which she lived.

Most of the children in Amy's neighborhood did not go to school. The few who did attend stayed off by themselves to avoid the ridicule of the other children.

Amy went out of her way to make friends. Her warm smile

radiated a friendly "hello" to every child she passed or sat next to at school. But the other children only returned her warm smiles and friendly greetings with unkind words and teasing. Some children even threw sticks at her.

Amy would feel very sad in her heart. She would run away and hide behind the school building. There was an old oak tree behind the school. Amy would sit at the base of the tree and cry.

"Why do people have to say such hurtful things to other people who are different? I don't understand why they have to be so cruel just because I don't live in a nice house like

they do, or have lots of toys."

She thought about Grandma's lessons. Grandma had talked about how some people judge others because they really don't know or understand them, or even take the time to know them.

"Everyone is different," said Grandma. People everywhere have different beliefs, different customs and ways of living.

"Some people are rich and others poor. Some people have brown skin; others yellow, red or white. It doesn't matter. People are people. Everyone is a part of God, and God is love. The more love we share, the happier place we can create right here on Earth."

Grandma's words were very wise. Yet for Amy, she just couldn't see how they could be applied to the situation she was in. It all seemed so unfair.

Amy began to take Lea to school with her for company. Each recess and lunch break, Amy would talk to Lea about how she wished everyone in the world could get along and accept each other no matter how they dress, what they look like or where they live. It really hurt Amy to feel so separate, so different so alone.

One girl in particular always went out of her way to make Amy sad from the hurtful things she would say to Amy.

Mary Ann was a very

unhappy, aggressive girl, large for her age. She seemed angry at the whole world and seemed to take her anger out on everyone who got in her way.

Amy could not understand why Mary Ann was so unhappy. She lived with her aunt in a big, two-story house on a hill in the city, complete with a beautiful swimming pool. She had her own bedroom filled with beautiful things. Mary Ann had a wardrobe of all the latest fashions. She seemed to have it all, Amy felt, yet Mary Ann was not happy.

One day, Amy was playing with Lea at her favorite spot under the oak tree. Mary Ann walked up to her and began her

usual jeering. Amy tried to ignore Mary Ann, which only made Mary Ann more angry.

"I want that doll!" shrieked Mary Ann in an angry tone. "Give it to me now! I want it now!"

Amy looked at her with fear in her eyes. But she stood her ground and said, "No, Mary Ann. Lea is my only toy. You have so many beautiful things. I don't understand why you want to pick on me and take my only doll from me."

"Because I don't like you. You're stupid. You don't deserve anything. You live over there in that dump."

Nothing made sense to Amy. She could not understand

a thing Mary Ann had said, other than she felt the tremendous anger Mary Ann was holding inside herself. But why?

Before she realized what was happening, Mary Ann suddenly grabbed Lea from Amy's arms. As quickly as Mary Ann had grabbed Lea, Lea's body came apart at the seams.

Amy felt helpless, but still she did not fight back. She was afraid that if she did, Mary Ann would hurt her next.

The school bell rang just in time to save Lea from further destruction, or Amy from having to deal further with Mary Ann.

Amy picked up Lea's parts and cradled them in her arms.

She did not return to the classroom, but ran home, sobbing loudly, hoping Mom could patch up Lea.

Mother tried to console Amy, but Amy could not hear her words through her tears. Before Amy could pull herself together, Mom had sewn Lea back together, good as new!

Lea was good as new, but Amy's heart still had a big hole right in the center of it.

Late that night a powerful earthquake struck the city, causing several explosions and a great fire which spread quickly in the high winds, destroying much of the town and the beautiful homes. The townspeople lost many of their prized possessions. Water sources were polluted with rubble. Food products were everywhere and most of the food had to be discarded. The people were devastated. They were confused and did not know what to do next.

The next morning, Amy's neighborhood was astir from the news of the quake. Amy, her family and neighbors walked into town to see what they could do to help.

They found that most of the city had burned to the ground. Many of the townspeople were sitting in the rubble where their homes once stood, shaking their heads, crying, wondering what to do next about the situation.

Amy's parents met a group of townspeople who were busily putting together a water station where everyone could get fresh, cold water to drink and cook with.

Amy's neighbors and family went back to their own homes to collect food, blankets and cooking items to share with the townspeople who had lost everything.

Soon, everyone was working together. It no longer seemed important which part of town anyone lived in, whether they were from this side of the tracks or the other.

What really mattered now was that everyone was helping

WATER

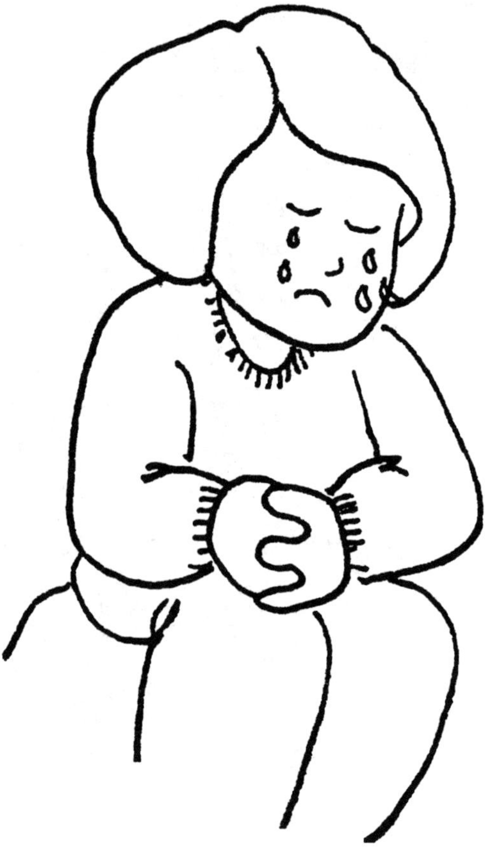

and sharing, working together to help patch up the broken lives.

Amy looked up toward the area where Mary Ann's aunt's beautiful home once stood. She saw Mary Ann, the girl who seemed to have everything, the bully, the angry little girl, sitting in front of what had been her home.

Amy walked up to Mary Ann, placed her hand on Mary Ann's shoulder, and smiled with tears filling her eyes.

"Oh, Amy. All my toys are gone – all of them. My beautiful Colleen – my beautiful doll – all gone! I have no clothes – they're all gone, too."

Mary Ann was crying

louder and louder. Somehow she no longer seemed a threat to Amy. Somehow, Mary Ann seemed like just another one of God's children who needed a little extra love and support.

Amy looked at Lea with a long, compassionate gaze. Remembering the rose – the symbol of love and compassion – and Grandma's lesson on love and sharing with others, Amy handed Lea over to Mary Ann.

"Here, Mary Ann. Lea is her name. I am going to let you keep her. Please take good care of her and give her lots of love, okay?"

Mary Ann looked at the cloth doll and suddenly burst

out in an even louder sobbing voice, "Amy, you can't do this! Lea is all you have! I had lots of things, but you only have this doll. If you give her to me, you will have nothing!"

"Oh, no," replied Amy. "I feel good about sharing Lea with you. I know you feel bad about the earthquake. Besides, Mommy can make me another doll.

"So, you keep Lea. I'll get another doll tomorrow." Amy choked back the tears.

Mary Ann reached over and grabbed Amy, giving her a big hug. Mary Ann's tears fell on Amy's shoulders leaving little wet spots. Amy smiled. A warm glow filled her heart and spread out upon her face.

Exhausted from their role in helping the townspeople recover their losses from the earthquake, Amy and her family slowly walked home. Amy decided not to tell her mother about Lea, but to wait until morning, after things quieted down a bit.

Amy climbed into her snug bed, pulling the quilt up to her chin. She tipped her head back to look at the picture of the red rose hanging on the wall. She noticed that the rose seemed different somehow. It seemed to have a very special glow about it, or maybe it was just her imagination.

Love . . . compassion . . . yes!

That's what it's all about. People sharing and caring for each other. Amy smiled.

Amy could see how the earthquake had brought the people of her town closer together. She felt it was sad that such a disaster was necessary to make people realize that all people are the same – equal – that all people are here to share the same beautiful Earth, that all people need to love and care for each other.

Amy cried softly for her loss and then realized the joy that her small gift had brought to Mary Ann. Yes, it felt good to share. It felt good to help others. With that thought, Amy fell asleep.

Shortly after Amy fell asleep, she became aware of a loving feeling all around her. She wasn't sure whether she was dreaming or not. Amy tried to open her eyes. Her eyes would not open.

A beautiful lady was now standing in Amy's inner vision. Golden light surrounded her body as she began to speak to Amy softly, lovingly, with great compassion: "Amy, you have given unselfishly to those who have hurt you. Your love is like a beacon of light shining down on and lighting the path of all who know you.

"You have learned a great lesson about love and sharing, that when you give from your

heart in a loving way, you receive back even more than you give out.

"We have both had to give up someone we love to make things better for everyone. I give you this message . . . your kindness shall not go unrewarded . . . you shall see. I leave you this one red rose as a symbol of my love for you, and the love that the Father in Heaven has for you.

"Never forget the special love that lives within you, and within each and every person on this Earth. Always share your love. Always be compassionate, no matter what the situation. Know you shall always be rewarded in ways far, far greater than you may ever expect.

"May God bless you. I give you my most sincere love and devotion. I am the Virgin Mary."

As the vision disappeared, Amy fell into a deep sleep.

To her surprise, as Amy awoke the next morning, at the end of her bed was one red rose! Was it a dream? Was the Virgin Mary really here, in this very room? Amy wasn't really sure what had happened, but it felt wonderful. She was all tingly inside.

In the next few weeks, the grateful townspeople joined together to share in the rebuilding of all that had been lost in the earthquake and fire. Amy's neighborhood was

given a new coat of paint. All the buildings were repaired until the whole neighborhood seemed to shine.

Everyone was sharing the most beautiful experience Amy had ever been a part of – helping one another, working together, no longer judging who was "better" than the other.

Amy's father was offered a job tending the local grocery store. Amy's mother had more sewing than she could handle. An extra bedroom was added to their small house, but Amy chose to let her mother use it as a sewing room.

"My place, my bedroom, is next to the fireplace. It is a very special place. Here

Grandma first taught me about the importance of sharing, of giving, of loving everyone equally. It was here that I saw that beautiful lady, the Virgin Mary. It was here that I received a very special gift, a gift of love – the one red rose."

As Amy spoke, someone knocked on the door. To her surprise, as Amy opened the door, she was greeted by the big, warm smile of Mary Ann. In Mary Ann's hand was a beautiful new doll, a doll even larger and more beautiful than Lea, more beautiful than any doll Amy had ever seen.

The doll seemed to glow, to send out a very special feeling of warmth and love. This feeling

seemed to fill all of Amy's house.

In the doll's hand was a single red rose. Amy suddenly remembered her vision, and the rose at the end of her bed.

As Mary Ann handed the doll back to Amy, she began to speak while choking back the tears, "Amy, this is for you. Thank you . . . I . . . I love you very much. Thank you for your sharing. You taught me something very special."

Amy smiled, lovingly cradling her new doll in her arms. Like soft little clouds drifting in a gentle breeze, the Virgin's words came into Amy's mind . . . "Amy, your kindness shall not go unrewarded . . . ."

"I love you, too, Mary Ann."

The two girls hugged each other tightly, tears of happiness streaming down their cheeks.

Amy looked up toward the heavens and whispered, "Thank you for this miracle of love. Thank you for everything."

Other Books by Leia Stinnett:

A Circle of Angels
The Twelve Universal Laws

The Little Angel Books Series:
The Angel Told Me to Tell You Good-bye
The Bridge Between Two Worlds
Color Me One
Crystals R for Kids
Exploring the Chakras
When the Earth Was New
Where Is God?
Who's Afraid of the Dark?

All My Angel Friends (Coloring Book)

About the Author

The '80s were a decade of self-discovery for Leia Stinnett after she began researching many different avenues of spirituality. In her profession as a graphic designer she had become restless, knowing there was something important she had to do outside the materiality of corporate America.

In August 1986 Leia had her first contact with Archangel Michael when he appeared in a physical form of glowing blue light. A voice said, "I am Michael. Together we will save the children."

In 1988 she was inspired by Michael to teach spiritual classes in Sacramento, California, the Circle of Angels. Through these classes she had the opportunity to work with learning-disabled children, children of abuse and those from dysfunctional homes.

Later Michael told her, "Together we are going to write the Little Angel Books." To date Leia and Michael have created thirteen Little Angel Books that present various topics of spiritual truths and principles. The books proved popular among adults as well as children.

The Circle of Angels classes have been introduced to several countries around the world and across the U.S., and Leia and her husband Douglas now have a teacher's manual and training program for people who wish to offer spiritual classes to children. Leia and Michael have been interviewed on Canadian Satellite TV and have appeared on NBC-TV's *Angels II – Beyond the Light,* which featured their Circle of Angels class and discussed their books and Michael's visit.

The angels have given Leia and Douglas a vision of a new educational system without competition or grades — one that supports love and positive self-esteem, honoring all children as the independent lights they are. Thus they are now writing a curriculum for the new "schools of light" and developing additional books and programs for children.